THE NEED TO KNOW LIBRARY™

EVERYTHING YOU NEED TO KNOW ABOUT
SEXUAL CONSENT

CARLA MOONEY

Rosen
YA™
New York

Published in 2018 by The Rosen Publishing Group, Inc.
29 East 21st Street, New York, NY 10010

Library of Congress Cataloging-in-Publication Data

Names: Mooney, Carla, 1970– author.
Title: Everything you need to know about sexual consent / Carla Mooney.
Description: New York : Rosen Publishing, 2018. | Series: The need to know library | Includes bibliographical references and index. | Audience: Grades 7–12.
Identifiers: LCCN 2017003222 | ISBN 9781508174127 (library-bound) | ISBN 9781508174103 (pbk.) | ISBN 9781508174110 (6-pack)
Subjects: LCSH: Sexual consent—Juvenile literature. | Sexual ethics—Juvenile literature. | Rape—Juvenile literature. | Youth—Sexual behavior—Juvenile literature.
Classification: LCC HQ32 .M647 2018 | DDC 176/.4—dc23
LC record available at https://lccn.loc.gov/2017003222

Manufactured in China

CONTENTS

INTRODUCTION

In May 2014, at an elite prep school in New Hampshire called St. Paul's School, eighteen-year-old Owen Labrie invited a fifteen-year-old female student to hang out. The meeting was part of a school tradition known as the senior salute, in which graduating seniors asked out younger students. The dates often led to sexual activity, anything from kissing to sex.

Labrie had a key to a mechanical room at the school and took the girl there. According to Labrie, the two kissed, fondled, and engaged in some sexual activity. He also claimed that their sexual activity was consensual.

However, the girl did not agree. She insisted that while she had initially agreed to some kissing and fondling, she had told Labrie to stop several times. He continued and went on to have sex with her. A few days later, the girl reported the encounter to the school. As required by law, the school reported the case to local law enforcement. After an investigation, prosecutors charged Labrie with felony sexual assault, along with several other charges.

The case against Labrie hinged on the issue of sexual consent. New Hampshire is one of the few states that does not require prosecutors to show force was used to prove sexual assault. At the 2015 trial, the girl testified that she felt like she was frozen

In 2015, eighteen-year-old Owen Labrie was tried in a criminal court like this one.

during the sexual encounter. Labrie claimed that he believed she gave consent because she did not stop his advances.

After hours of deliberations, the jury found Labrie not guilty of the most serious charge, felony sexual assault. They convicted him on several lesser misdemeanor charges, including having sex with a minor and soliciting minors for sex using the internet. As punishment, Labrie served one year in a county jail. He also was required to register as a sex offender for the computer crime, which he later appealed.

In recent years, communities and schools across the United States have been shocked by reports of rape and sexual assault. In a September 2015 survey by the Association of American Universities, more than 23 percent of female college students said they had experienced some form of unwanted sexual contact, which ranged from kissing and touching to rape. The contact occurred by force or threat of force, or while the women were incapacitated by alcohol or drugs. "The results warrant the attention and concern of everybody in our community," said Drew Faust, president of Harvard University in 2015. "Sexual assault is intolerable, and we owe it to one another to confront it openly, purposefully, and effectively. This is *our* problem."

As part of the effort to end sexual assault, awareness and understanding of sexual consent has become an increasingly important issue across the country. Colleges and communities have begun to discuss sexual consent and redefine what exactly consent means. Many have started education programs to teach students about affirmative consent, healthy relationships, and respect, as well as what sexual assault is and how to report it.

CHAPTER ONE

WHAT IS SEXUAL CONSENT?

In most situations, society understands consent, but when it comes to sex, that is not necessarily the case. According to a 2015 poll by the Washington Post-Kaiser Family Foundation, college students have different ideas about what consent is. In the poll, at least 40 percent of students said that certain unspoken actions—such as nodding, taking off clothes, or getting a condom—counted as consent for sex. However, another 40 percent of students said that those same actions were not consent.

In a 2015 article in the *Washington Post*, Holly Copeland, a twenty-two-year-old graduate of Indiana State University, said she believes that nods should not be considered consent because they can be misunderstood and manipulated. She also believes that taking off one's clothes is not a green light for sex. "If a stripper is taking off her clothes, does that mean she's consenting for the patron to touch her? No. There's a line there," said Copeland.

Most people agree that sexual consent is a voluntary agreement between two people to participate in sexual activity, specifically by saying yes. It may

The woman on the left might be nodding, showing her consent to or agreement with something. Her facial expression shows that she appears to be enjoying the conversation they are having.

seem pretty simple, but in real life, that is not always the case.

AFFIRMATIVE CONSENT

For many years, "no means no" was the socially acceptable standard for sexual consent. A person who did not want to participate in sexual activity, or let such activity go any further once started, could simply say no. But under this definition, not saying anything could be interpreted as giving consent. It also put the burden on victims of sexual assault, making it their responsibility to show that they tried to resist.

In recent years, some schools and communities have begun to redefine what sexual consent is. They define consent as showing active and enthusiastic agreement. Instead of "no means no," sexual consent is now defined as "yes means yes." They hope that this new consent standard will prevent sexual assault.

Affirmative consent occurs when a person gives a clear, affirmative yes before engaging in sexual activity. Therefore,

A teen asks if she can borrow her friend's phone. Her friend gives it to her freely.

silence or not saying no to sexual activity does not count as consent. In a 2015 *New York Times* article, University at Albany (NY) sex educator Carol Stenger, said that affirmative consent is like borrowing a cell phone. "You wouldn't just take it. You'd ask for it first," Stenger said.

Affirmative consent must also be voluntary. Affirmative consent can only be given with enthusiasm and excitement about sexual activity. If an inexpressive partner just lets it happen, that is not consent. There also can be no pressure or manipulation to have sex on the part of the partner who is seeking consent, or that is invalid.

Getting consent is not a one-time thing. Two people who want to engage in sexual activity need to get consent every time and for every act because sexual consent is everyone's responsibility. "Consent needs to be something where both parties are actively saying yes, rather than not saying no," said Alan Bowers, a student at Utah State University, in a June 2015 *Washington Post* article. "It is completely realistic for both parties to say, 'Yes, let's do this.' I don't see any situation where that wouldn't be possible."

That doesn't mean there's no longer a place for saying no. A person can say no to certain sexual activity at any time. Offering consent also might mean saying yes to one specific activity, but not to others. Timing is also important. If two people agree to have sex today, that does not mean they should not reaffirm consent in the future. It also doesn't mean that the initial offer of affirmative consent cannot be explicitly revoked.

INFORMED CONSENT

Getting sexual consent must involve discussing certain parts of an encounter, and important aspects of one's sexual history. Before sexual activity, a person must tell his or her partner about any sexually transmitted diseases that he or she has. Omitting this information can be considered manipulation, since there is a chance that knowing that someone's partner has an STD would influence the decision to take part in sexual contact. Such a revelation also could influence the decision whether or not to use protection. Not mentioning STDs up front can also lead to criminal and civil charges, and all of the penalties that come with them. Failing to disclose HIV, in particular, is treated as a special case in many US states. A person who is accused of hiding an HIV-positive status may face attempted murder charges if they knowingly infect a sexual partner.

Similarly, sexual partners should be honest about how sexually active they have been, including how many other partners they have had, how long ago these relationships were, and whether or not protection was involved. The risk that comes with not being forthcoming is twofold. Someone who has multiple sexual partners at the same time is at greater risk for being infected with STDs if they aren't using protection. Any sexual activity at all has a risk that is worth investigating, unless that person makes it clear that he or she has determined through medical testing that there is nothing to worry about. The second risk is that not establishing the exclusivity of the partners' relationship can lead to hurt feelings if there is no honest agreement about what each person wants.

Discussing protection is also important. Knowing who should bring the condoms or if another other form

CALIFORNIA HIGH SCHOOLS TEACH AFFIRMATIVE CONSENT

In June 2016, the California state legislature passed a law that brings learning about affirmative consent to high school students. The first of its kind in the country, the law requires all California school districts that have health class as a graduation requirement to include a lesson on affirmative consent. The schools should focus on teaching students that sexual consent is only given when yes is clearly communicated. The lesson also must teach students that being silent or not saying no is not consent. The new law passed the legislature unopposed and took effect on January 1, 2017.

"I think it's very important for students to learn about consent in school because it will prepare you for life," said Los Angeles high school student Taylor Silverstein in a June 2016 *Seventeen* magazine article. "This kind of knowledge is extremely powerful and important."

of birth control is being used is a discussion for both partners. Not only would protection prevent the sharing of STDs, it would also prevent any unwanted pregnancies from occurring. But be aware that some protection is more effective than others at preventing both the transmission of STDs and pregnancy.

CONSENT AND ALCOHOL AND DRUGS

Alcohol and drugs can complicate sex because they impair a person's judgment. They also affect a person's ability to communicate. A person who is drunk may agree to sexual activity that he or she would not have when sober, and that person may not be able to communicate no effectively. A person who is under the influence of drugs or alcohol may also have trouble understanding nonverbal cues and might not be able to see that a partner is not interested in continuing sexual activity. To make it even more difficult, many people find it hard to tell if a person has had too much to drink.

In some situations, it is possible for a person who is intoxicated to give consent as long as it is clear, affirmative, and voluntary. Other times, a person may be so drunk or high that he or she is incapacitated. An incapacitated person cannot give consent. Some signs of incapacitation include not being able to speak coherently, getting confused about basic facts, being unable to walk without assistance, or passing out. Exploiting a person who is incapacitated by alcohol or drugs is never acceptable. When in doubt, don't have sex.

SEXUAL ASSAULT

Sexual assault is a crime that involves unwanted contact of a physical nature. That contact may include but is not limited to touching, fondling, or kissing. Assault can also occur when someone uses force or pressure—either physical or emotional—to get someone to perform a sexual act. In every case, sexual assault is not the victim's fault.

These two teens are having an argument. Coercing or threatening a partner into agreeing to participate in an activity, sexual or otherwise, is not acceptable.

It is possible for sexual assault to occur in the case of one or many strangers attacking a victim, but it also may occur with people who already know each other and who may even be in a relationship. Men and women of all ages, races, and sexual orientations can be victims of sexual assault. The location for where it may occur is similarly unlimited. While most victims of sexual assault are female, one out of every five victims is male.

Understanding what sexual consent is and making sure it is given during all encounters is an important part of any romantic relationship. Getting sexual consent can make sure every sexual encounter is a good experience for both partners. When in doubt, it is best to take a moment to ask.

MYTHS AND FACTS

MYTH: A person can guarantee avoiding sexual assault as long as he or she follows certain guidelines, such as acting or dressing conservatively, not going out at night alone, and not drinking alcohol or doing drugs.

FACT: Sexual assault can happen to anyone at any time. When someone is motivated to commit sexual assault against a stranger, they are more likely motivated by an internal urge to control and meet their own desires than an external factor like someone's appearance. Also, it's a crime that occurs more often between people who know each other already. The fact of opportunity may be more important than sexual attractiveness. In either case, a date rape drug like Rohypnol is not too picky about whether it goes into an alcoholic drink, a soft drink, or water. The drinker usually isn't aware their drink has been drugged, and that their safety has intentionally been compromised. In other words, no matter what you do "right," someone else's bad intentions can take away your safety.

MYTH: Sexual assault is rare.

FACT: According to the National Institute of Alcohol Abuse and Alcoholism, 25 percent of American women have experienced sexual assault, including rape. That's one in four. The National Sexual Violence Resource Center notes one in five women and one in sixteen men are sexually assaulted while in college. These projections, taken from real data, demonstrate that there is a high chance that everyone knows someone who has been sexually assaulted.

(continued on the next page)

(continued from the previous page)

MYTH: Once a person consents to sexual activity, saying no is not an option.

FACT: Yes, it is. It is possible to revoke consent after giving it, regardless of the reason, even while in the middle of sex or some other act to which consent was previously given. Also, giving consent for an initial sexual encounter doesn't mean that a person has given consent for all potential encounters in the future.

CHAPTER TWO

SEXUAL CONSENT ON CAMPUS

Sexual assault is a pervasive problem on college campuses across the United States. According to a 2015 survey conducted by *The Washington Post* and the Kaiser Family Foundation, one in five women on campus have been sexually assaulted. Many others have been the victims of attempted sexual assault or suspect that someone had sexual contact with them while they were unable to consent. Some say they were unwillingly participants in sex because of verbal threats or promises. And it is not just women who are victims. The survey found that 7 percent of men experienced unwanted sexual incidents in college. Two-thirds of the survey's participants (both sexes) said they were drinking alcohol just before the unwanted sexual contact.

REPORTING AND NOT REPORTING

Sexual assault on campus often goes unreported. According to the 2015 survey by *The Washington*

Students at a college party hang out with friends and have a few beers. Drinking alcohol can impair a person's judgment and make that person vulnerable to unwanted sexual contact.

Post and the Kaiser Family Foundation, only 11 percent of victims reported a sexual assault to police or college authorities. Many victims do not want to report the crime because they fear how others will treat them. More than four in ten women said it was very or somewhat likely that a woman would be criticized by other students if she reported an assault.

Although most victims do not report an assault to campus authorities, the majority of victims do tell someone. They might confide in a trusted friend or family member. Often, sharing the event can help the victim or an assault heal.

Some victims choose not to report a sexual assault on campus because they fear being made fun of or criticized by other students and faculty.

In other cases revealed in that 2015 survey, a friend's lack of understanding about consent and sexual assault can cause more problems. A nineteen-year-old student at the University of Michigan got drunk at a fraternity party and blacked out. She believed that she was sexually assaulted while she was unable to consent. She chose not to report the assault to authorities because she feared backlash from the fraternity. Instead, she chose to confide in a male friend. She was stunned when he said that there was a difference between regret over having sex while being drunk and being raped. His reaction ended their friendship.

CHANGING POLICIES AND LEGISLATION TO THE AFFIRMATIVE CONSENT STANDARD

To prevent sexual assault, many colleges have started changing their sexual misconduct policies. Instead of the old "no means no" rules, many schools are adopting affirmative consent or "yes means yes" standards for sexual contact. An estimated 1,500 colleges and universities use some form of affirmative consent in their sexual assault policies.

Supporters applaud the changes. They say that affirmative consent is a valuable tool against sexual assault. It also helps students understand the difference between consensual sex and sex that is forced or coerced. Schools are updating websites to explain the new policies. They also have increased student outreach and education programs. In an October 2015 article in the *Chicago Tribune*, Molly McLay, assistant director at the University of Illinois Women's Resources Center, said, "Sexual violence is a huge issue in our society, and we hope these efforts open up a broad network of support for those who feel like they have nowhere else to turn."

States are also changing their standards. In 2014, California became the first state to pass legislation that requires colleges and universities that receive state financial aid to adopt an affirmative consent policy. Furthermore, the California law states that:

> ... lack of protest or resistance does not mean consent, nor does silence mean consent. Affirmative consent must be ongoing throughout a sexual activity and

New York governor Andrew Cuomo (*center*) signs affirmative consent legislation in 2015 while several supporters gather around him.

can be revoked at any time. The existence of a dating relationship between the persons involved, or the fact of past sexual relations between them, should never by itself be assumed to be an indicator of consent.

Dana Bolger, cofounder of a survivor-run campaign to end sexual violence called Know Your IX, said that the bill is a significant victory for assault survivors and all students. She hopes that other states will follow California's example and pass their own affirmative consent laws.

In 2015, New York became the second state to pass affirmative consent legislation. Under New York's law, sexual consent requires an affirmative agreement between two people. When signing the law, Governor Andrew Cuomo said that the policy would help end sexual assault on campus.

DENIAL OF DUE PROCESS

While most people support efforts to stop sexual assault on campus, some are concerned that affirmative consent laws and policies are not enforceable and violate the civil rights of the accused. "No one denies that consent is required for sexual activity, but the problem is when the burden of proof shifts to the accused to prove his or her innocence," said Samantha Harris, a lawyer with the Foundation for Individual Rights in Education, in an October 2015 article in the Chicago Tribune. "It's an overcorrection."

C. D. Mock became an advocate for young men after his son was accused of sexual assault during his junior year of college. After attending a party with a classmate, Mock's son said that he and a woman had consensual sex. The next day, the son was blindsided when the woman he had been with accused him of rape. "He was just blown away," Mock said in a 2016 interview posted on ABC News.com. "He didn't know how to react because he just didn't—that wasn't what he expected."

At first the university dismissed the charges against Mock's son. A few weeks later, the school reversed its ruling and found him responsible for the assault. A year later, a local court cleared Mock's son and ruled that the school had improperly shifted the burden of proof onto him. Mock warned that affirmative consent laws placed a nearly impossible burden to prove innocence on those accused. "Due process has gone out the window for young men," Mock said. "We need to be careful here. You are guilty until you prove yourself innocent, which is the way it is today."

CAMPUS EDUCATION EFFORTS

Colleges and universities across the country have implemented programs for new students to learn about consent, assault, and intervention. The time between the beginning of the school year and Thanksgiving is called the red zone. Experts consider this period to be the most likely time for sexual violence on college campuses. To prevent incidences on campus, particularly during this time frame, many schools now require all incoming students to attend sexual consent and assault workshops. Some schools offer the training online, before the students even arrive on campus. Also, many

A student uses a tablet to complete an online sexual consent training course. It is likely that his college requires students to complete sexual consent training before they arrive on campus.

colleges are holding workshops and events throughout the school year to reinforce the initial training.

The new training is a reaction to several high-profile assault cases that have drawn the country's attention to the problem of sexual assault. "What used to be OK and tolerated years ago isn't now," said Jim McHugh, associate vice president for athletic affairs and Title IX coordinator at California Lutheran University, in an August 2016 article in the Ventura County Star. "When I was in college, all this was going on, and we never heard about it."

At Trinity College in Hartford, Connecticut, Jonathan Kalin speaks to freshman students about the importance of consent. Kalin is the founder of Party with Consent, an organization that promotes healthy interactions between men and women at college parties across U.S. campuses. Kalin came up with the idea for Party with Consent after seeing another college's students wearing T-shirts with a Party with Sluts logo. In college at the time, Kalin decided to turn the logo into something with a more positive message.

At Trinity, Kalin's lecture is part of the college's mandatory sexual assault curriculum for freshman. Following the lecture, students are invited to an actual "party with consent" that has bands, an open bar, and bowls of condoms with "Did you ask consent?" labels.

"In my experience, when you ask men on college campuses where they learned about consent, they sort of look at you blankly and say, 'What do you mean?'" Kalin said in a January 2016 New York Times article. "This is meant to be like a pre-intro intro course. Hopefully it's a gateway to a larger conversation."

THE IT'S ON US CAMPAIGN

Awareness and educational programs for the general public are shining a light on campus sexual assault and the issue of sexual consent. In 2014, President Barack Obama and the Center for American Progress launched the It's On Us initiative, a public awareness campaign to put an end to sexual assault on college campuses. It's On Us asks all Americans to make a personal commitment to get involved and help end campus sexual assault. The campaign aims to make people think differently about sexual assault and inspire every person to make it his or her responsibility to prevent it.

Various celebrities, athletes, student leaders, media platforms, and others have partnered with the campaign to help spread its message. Public service announcements feature stars such as Zoe Saldana, Josh Hutcherson, Jon Hamm, and Connie Britton speaking about the importance and necessity of sexual consent.

In 2016, Vice President Joe Biden teamed up with recording artist and sexual assault survivor Lady Gaga to support It's On Us. Biden introduced Lady Gaga at the Oscars before she performed her Oscar-nominated song "Til It Happens To You." The song was written and recorded for *The Hunting Ground*, a 2015 documentary about sexual assault on campus. During his

Vice President Joe Biden speaks at Marine Corps Base Hawaii in 2011. He also travels to institutions of learning as part of his work with It's On Us.

introduction, Biden spoke about the It's On Us campaign and the importance of making a commitment to
end sexual assault. After the show, the It's On Us campaign received a significant spike in pledges.

In an interview with Billboard.com, Biden spoke about
his work with It's On Us and his travels to colleges and
universities across America on behalf of the organization. One of the most powerful moments he experienced
occurred after an event at the University of Illinois in
2015. Biden told the interviewer how a woman who had
attended the event had later come forward to report an
incident of sexual assault by a former boyfriend. "She
said she was compelled to act after attending the rally,"
Biden said. Her case was taken up by state and local
authorities. The ex wound up being charged with additional accounts of criminal sexual assault, based on the
accusations of two other former girlfriends.

CHAPTER THREE

SEXUAL CONSENT AND THE LAW

In a country as big as the United States, the law takes on varying perspectives because each state offers different definitions and guidelines for what is sexual assault and consent, as well as how to punish those convicted of a sex crime. It's important to understand how those factors can impact a victim who wants to seek justice after being violated. People should check their local state laws if they have any specific questions.

THE ROLE OF CONSENT

In the United States, the landscape for seeking justice for sexual violence is a bumpy one. Rebecca O'Connor, the Rape, Incest, and Abuse National Network (RAINN) vice president for public policy, wrote, "We know that the legal definitions for terms like rape, sexual assault, and sexual abuse vary from state to state." A victim in one state may not be defined as such in another, from a legal standpoint. Even so, sexual assault usually means any crime in which an offender sexually touches the victim in an unwanted and offensive way.

Sexual assault crimes can range from groping to attempted rape. Rape is defined as forced oral, vaginal, or anal penetration by a body part or an object. Some states separate different acts into different crimes, while others combine them together into a single category. Also, states can have different sentencing guidelines for offenders convicted of sexual assault.

Consent is an important part in determining whether or not a sexual act is a crime. Most states agree that any sexual contact without consent is a crime. But just as sexual assault is treated differently from state to state, there also is a lack of consensus regarding the legal definition of consent from one state to the next. For example, Florida law defines consent as being "intelligent, knowing, and voluntary." If coerced submission occurs, there is no consent, so failing to resist an offender physically is not consent. In contrast, Massachusetts law does not specifically define consent at all except in cases involving minors. In a sexual assault case, instead of describing it as offering consent, the law assesses whether the offender compelled the victim to submit by force or by the threat of injury.

In general, there are three main factors that states consider when determining if there was consent. First, they examine affirmative consent. They ask questions regarding whether or not the person communicated, either through clear actions or words, that he or she agreed to specific sexual activity. If not, consent was not given. Second, consent must be freely given. The person must have offered consent without being induced, coerced, or threatened. Finally, the state looks at whether or not the person had the capacity to

A person who is sleeping or passed out does not have the capacity to consent to sexual activity.

consent. Capacity to consent is the legal ability to give consent. In some situations, people may not have the capacity to consent. Even if they say yes, there is no consent.

CAPACITY TO CONSENT

A person's capacity to consent, or to agree in a manner that is acceptable by law, depends on several factors. Since the definition of consent varies by state, so, too, do these factors.

Age is one important factor. Every state has an age of consent. To consent to sexual activity, a person must be the stated age or older. If the person is not of age, he or she does not have the capacity to consent.

Another factor is whether or not the person is vulnerable or has a physical or developmental disability. Some vulnerable adults, such as the elderly or sick, do not have the capacity to consent. In a similar way, a person with a developmental disability, traumatic brain injury, or physical disability may not be able to consent. People who are sleeping or unconscious cannot give consent. Likewise, those who are drunk or high on drugs may not have the capacity to consent. If the state determines that a person did not have the capacity to consent, the state can charge the accused with a crime.

In other cases, the relationship between the victim and alleged perpetrator can affect the capacity to consent. Sexual activity between a teacher and a student or a coach and an athlete can be a crime. Most states find that the victim in these situations does not have the capacity to consent because the other person is in a position of authority.

In 2015, Megan Batykefer, a rowing coach at North Allegheny High School in Pennsylvania, was found guilty of felony institutional sexual assault for having sex with an eighteen-year-old student. Batykefer's attorney unsuccessfully argued that the sexual relationship was consensual and the student, who was eighteen years old at the time, was over Pennsylvania's legal age of consent of sixteen. However, because the rowing coach was in a position of authority over the student, the court ruled that the sexual relationship

A school sports team—a rowing team, for example—creates a situation in which an adult, the coach, is in a position of power over minors and possibly other adults. This power adds to the harm of a sex crime.

was a crime. In Pennsylvania, age does not matter when there is sexual contact between an employee of a school and a student, so even if the student consents to sexual activity, it is still a crime. The judge sentenced her to eight to twenty-three months in jail. Also, Batykefer lost her job as a rowing coach, as well as her teaching license.

A FINE LINE

In some situations, it is easy to tell that a sexual crime took place. When a perpetrator drugs a victim until he or she passes out and then has sex with that victim, most people consider it a crime. Because the victim is passed out and unresponsive, the perpetrator had to know that he or she was unable to consent. In these circumstances, most people agree that a crime was committed.

Other times, the legal question is not so clear. Some states require that a victim be substantially impaired, and also that the perpetrator know that the victim's ability to resist or consent is substantially impaired. According to the Ohio Court of Appeals:

> (T)here can be a fine, fuzzy, and subjective line between intoxication and impairment. Every alcohol consumption does not lead to a substantial impairment. Additionally, the waters become even murkier when reviewing whether a defendant knew, or should have known, that someone was impaired rather than merely intoxicated. Of course, there are times when it would be apparent to all onlookers that an individual is substantially impaired, such as intoxication to the point of unconsciousness. On the other hand, a person who is experiencing an alcohol induced blackout may walk, talk, and fully perform ordinary functions without others being able to tell that he is "blacked out."

In other states, the law only requires the victim to be incapacitated and unable to consent to sexual activity. The prosecution does not have to prove that the suspect knew that the victim could not give consent.

REPORTING A SEXUAL CRIME

After a sexual assault or rape, many people do not know how to react. They may be hurt physically. They may feel emotionally wrecked and unsure what to do. Some people choose to report the crime to law enforcement. Reporting a crime is an individual decision. Many people who decide to report to law enforcement believe that it is the first step toward justice and making an offender accountable for his or her actions.

There are several ways to report a sexual assault, and these are not mutually exclusive:

- Call 911 to get immediate help.
- Contact the local or campus police department.
- Go to a nearby hospital or medical center and report the crime to a medical professional.
- Call the National Sexual Assault Hotline at (800) 656-HOPE (4673) to be connected to a local sexual assault service provider, who can help navigate the process of getting help and reporting to law enforcement.

In most communities, there are law enforcement officers who are specially trained to help sexual assault victims. Many police departments have a Sexual Assault Response Team (SART), a group that provides a coordinated response to sexual assault. Team members include medical personnel, police, and local sexual assault service providers. Working together, the team organizes the investigation and helps communication among all agencies involved.

In thirty-four states and the District of Columbia, there is a time limit for a person to report a sexual assault crime. This limit is called the statute of limitations. It varies by state, type of crime, victim's age, and other factors. For example, Colorado's statute of limitations on sexual assault is ten years. In Connecticut, it is only five years.

If a person has been raped, he or she may decide to get a sexual assault forensic exam, using what is known as a rape kit. A sexual assault forensic exam collects DNA evidence from a victim's body, clothes, and other personal belongings. A victim does not always have to report the assault to have the exam. He

A sexual assault forensic exam collects physical and DNA evidence from a victim's body, clothing, and other possessions. That evidence then needs to be tested to confirm the details of a sexual assault.

or she can choose to safely store the evidence if the victim decides to report the assault in the future.

WHAT TO EXPECT FROM LAW ENFORCEMENT

Once a person reports a sexual assault, he or she needs to talk to law enforcement. Knowing what to expect can help a person feel more comfortable and in control. The process may take a few hours. The victim may talk to law enforcement once or there may be several interviews. Any discussions should be done in private, away from other people. Law enforcement may ask the same question repeatedly or in slightly different ways. They do this because repeating a question can help victims remember a detail that they forgot earlier. It's normal for some questions to make a person feel uncomfortable. Remembering that the law enforcement officer is a trained professional and is ready to listen can help reduce a person's discomfort.

Because the process can take some time, victims can ask for a break. They also can ask to have a trained advocate or trusted family member or friend with them for the interview. These people can provide support to the victim during the interview process.

When investigating the assault, law enforcement has several goals. First, they attempt to prove lack of consent. Most sexual assaults are committed by a person who already knows the victim. Therefore, the culprit's identity is often already known. Proving there was no consent becomes key to prosecuting the case.

Law enforcement also tries to gather evidence to dispute any arguments that could be made to defend the suspect. They collect and document evidence that the sexual contact was not consensual. They collect and preserve DNA samples from the victim and suspect and any other physical evidence from the crime scene. They interview witnesses and document their statements. They document evidence that there was no consent or that fear, force, threats, or coercion were used to get the victim to consent. Also, they document if the victim was unable to consent at the time of the encounter.

With all of this information, law enforcement prepares a report. The report includes a detailed description of the assault, whether there was any evidence of premeditation, signs of force, lack of consent, a time line of the assault, and the victim's response.

PRESSING CHARGES

After reporting an assault to law enforcement, police can decide if they want to move forward with the investigation by pressing charges. The final decision on whether or not to charge a suspect with a crime is made by the state. The prosecution team evaluates the evidence documented by law enforcement. If they believe they have enough evidence to prove that a crime occurred, they will arrest the suspect and charge him or her with sexual assault. If the prosecution does not feel they have enough evidence to prove that a suspect is guilty, they may decide not to press charges.

Usually the victim is required to testify or be further involved in some way, but in some rare cases, a prosecutor may decide to charge a suspect with assault even if the victim does not want to be involved. Outside of criminal court, a victim may choose to file a lawsuit in civil court against a suspect.

Many sexual assault cases are not settled in court. Instead, they are resolved with a plea bargain. A plea bargain is an agreement in which the accused agrees to plead guilty to a crime in return for a reduced penalty or lighter sentence. In a plea bargain, the victim does not have to testify in court.

GOING TO TRIAL

When the assailant doesn't agree to a plea

Police will interview the victim, the accused, and any potential witnesses when a crime like sexual assault is brought to their attention.

bargain, the case goes to trial in a criminal court. The prosecuting attorney represents the state in the case against the defendant. The prosecution usually asks the victim to testify in court because the victim's testimony is likely the strongest evidence they have. When testifying in court, a witness or victim will be asked to make an oath to tell the truth before being asked several questions in front of a judge and a jury. A witness or victim's testimony will consist of answers to questions

TIPS FOR TESTIFYING

Although it can be very stressful to testify at trial, that testimony is often an important part of the prosecution's case against the defendant. The following tips can help victims and witnesses stay calm during their testimony:

• Take brief pauses and ask for a short break if overwhelmed.
• Stay hydrated; bring a water bottle and take regular sips of water.
• Keep calm by pausing and slowing down when feeling angry or frustrated.
• Look at the person who is asking the questions.
• Tell the truth. If a victim does not remember something, he or she needs to say so.
• Answer the question, but no more; don't offer additional information without being asked to do so.
• Victims should ask for clarification when they don't understand what a question means. Ask the attorney to clarify or reword the question.

from the prosecutor about the crime and the circumstances surrounding it. In the case of questioning a victim, the prosecutor often reviews these questions with the victim in advance and helps that person to get ready to testify.

The victim may also have to answer questions from the defense attorney. This lawyer, who represents the defendant, has the task of proving that the defendant is not guilty of a crime. In some states, there are laws about what lawyers can and cannot ask the victim while he or she is testifying. For example, in some states, the defense cannot ask the victim about prior sexual history.

Although it can be terrifying to testify in court, some victims receive support from an advocate they bring with them to court. An advocate can help them during the trial and make the process less scary and stressful.

Once all the witnesses and the victim have testified and all the evidence has been presented, the judge or jury will decide if the defendant is guilty or not guilty of breaking the law. If the defendant is found guilty of sexual assault or any supplementary charges related to one or multiple specific incidents, the case goes to a judge for sentencing. The penalties for sexual assault and other related crimes vary by state. For example, in California, a defendant convicted of sexual assault may receive a sentence of twenty-five to forty-eight months in prison, along with a fine. In New York, the judge can set a sentence within a range of a minimum of one to two years and a maximum of seven years. The defendant can serve the minimum or the

A jury listens intently as the prosecutors and defense attorneys present evidence at a trial.

entire term, based on his or her behavior in prison and other factors.

Sometimes the judge or jury finds a defendant not guilty, but a not guilty verdict does not necessarily mean that the defendant is innocent. Instead, a not guilty verdict may mean that the court did not have enough evidence to find the defendant guilty beyond a reasonable doubt. Failure to convict also shields the accused from further criminal prosecution in the matter of that specific incident. This is called double jeopardy.

CHAPTER FOUR

HEALING FROM SEXUAL ASSAULT AND RAPE

After a sexual assault, many people do not know what to do. A person may be hurt physically. They may be emotionally upset and confused. They might want to tell someone but don't know whom to tell or how to start. There are many places for survivors of sexual assault to get help. Knowing where to go and whom to turn to is the first step toward healing.

SAFETY AND MEDICAL CARE

After being assaulted, a person should immediately seek a safe place and call someone who is trustworthy to come get him or her. If a person is seriously injured or in immediate danger, it is a better option to call 911 as soon as possible.

After a sexual assault, a survivor may need medical care. Local hospitals and health facilities have doctors and other trained personnel who can care for people who are sexually attacked. They will treat any injuries sustained during the assault. They also can check for and treat any injuries that are not easily seen. Medical treatment can also screen a person for sexually transmitted diseases or infections and assess whether or not there is a risk of pregnancy. Getting medical care as soon as possible can help avoid more serious problems in the future. Medical professionals can refer victims to other resources and services to help them recover.

No one should have to worry about going to the hospital alone. If someone does not have a trusted friend or family member who can come with him or her, he or she can call a local sexual assault service provider. The provider can send a trained advocate to go with the survivor to the hospital. The advocate can explain each step of the process to the survivor and provide support throughout the experience.

This woman is calling someone to help her escape from a dangerous situation.

HOTLINE FOR HELP

Immediately after a sexual assault, survivors can call the National Sexual Assault Hotline at 800- 656-4673 for help. The hotline connects people with a trained staff member from a local sexual assault service provider. This staff member can walk a person through the steps to get help. They can direct a person to local hospitals and health facilities that provide care in such instances They can also send a trained advocate to accompany and support the survivor. The hotline can also provide referrals for local resources such as counselors and support groups. Callers can also ask questions about basic medical concerns and get information about local sexual assault laws. All calls to the hotline are completely confidential.

Trained staff members answer calls to a sexual assault hotline to help callers navigate the next steps they should take and find local resources to help them.

SEXUAL ASSAULT FORENSIC EXAM

While at the hospital, a survivor may choose to have a sexual assault forensic exam. Using a rape kit, doctors collect evidence of a sexual assault from a survivor's body, clothing, and other personal belongings. In most cases, DNA evidence should be collected within seventy-two hours of an assault. Before the exam, the victim should try to avoid doing anything that would damage the evidence, such as bathing, showering, going to the bathroom, changing clothes, combing his or her hair, and other general cleaning.

Specially trained professionals perform these exams. If a health facility does not have a staff member trained to perform the exam, survivors can call the National Sexual Assault Hotline to help them locate the nearest facility with trained personnel.

The health professional performing the exam will usually begin by talking to the person reporting the assault. They will ask him or her about their current medical health and recent consensual sexual activity. They also will ask a detailed description of what happened during the assault. Although these questions may feel uncomfortable or invasive, they will help the professional identify all the areas where potential evidence or injury may be found.

Next, health professionals will closely examine the survivor. The exam may include a full-body examination. They also may take samples of blood, urine, and hair. They may swab different areas on the survivor's body, take pictures to document the survivor's injuries, and collect the survivor's clothing for forensic testing.

Any other physical evidence found during the exam will be collected and packaged. If at any time a survivor is feeling uncomfortable, he or she can stop, pause, or skip a step in the exam. It is the survivor's decision.

The exam itself may take a few hours. Many survivors find it comforting to have someone to support them during the exam. This may be a trustworthy friend or family member. It can also be a trained sexual assault advocate. Anyone present during an exam may be called as a witness if the survivor decides to report the crime to law enforcement.

There are special considerations with regard to reporting. If the survivor is a minor, the person performing the exam may be required by law to report it to law enforcement. It is likely that law enforcement will alert the minor's parents of the incident. Also, whatever a survivor chooses, it is important to reiterate that there is a chance that a time limit on reporting a sexual assault crime exists, depending on state laws.

HEALING AND SELF-CARE

Although sexual assault is never the victim's fault, survivors often feel like they did something wrong. Many sexual assault survivors experience symptoms of post-traumatic stress disorder (PTSD). They may experience anxiety and depression. They may have nightmares or flashbacks to the assault. They may lose interest in activities that they used to enjoy and avoid places and situations that remind them of the assault.

Talking to a trained mental health counselor can help victims of sexual assault heal and learn to deal with the lasting trauma of the experience.

Some survivors find that psychotherapy helps them heal from a sexual assault. During a therapy session, the survivor talks to a trained counselor about his or her feelings and learns strategies for dealing with them. Strategies include coping skills and stress management. They can also talk about thoughts and feelings that they are not comfortable discussing with friends and family. There is no specific time line for developing the tools someone needs to cope, so a survivor should take part in therapy until the task of healing is complete.

Self-care is another important part of healing from a sexual assault. Eating well, exercising, and getting

Working out can help a person relieve symptoms of stress and help a person better manage depression.

enough sleep are important physical aspects of self-care. Exercise can relieve stress and fatigue and combat depression. Emotional self-care is also critical for long-term healing. In addition to therapy, some people find that certain activities such as art or writing can help them express their thoughts and feelings and release stress. Some people find that meditation or yoga release stress and promote a general sense of well-being.

Surrounding oneself with supportive people is another important part of long-term recovery. Support may come from family, friends, a therapist, or a support group of people who have experienced a sexual assault. Many people find that joining a support group and meeting others with similar experiences help in their recovery.

Recovery and healing from sexual assault takes time and effort. However, recovery is possible. People who experience a sexual assault are not alone because there is help and support available to them.

10 GREAT QUESTIONS TO ASK A COLLEGE SEXUAL ASSAULT COUNSELOR

1. What is the school policy on sexual assault and violence?
2. What sexual consent education do you provide to students, staff, and faculty, and is it mandatory?
3. What sexual assault prevention programs does the school have in place, and how often are they active?
4. How many sexual assaults were reported on and off campus in the past year? What about for each of the past ten years?
5. Do you have a school office dedicated to sexual assault prevention and response that coordinates the response to a sexual assault report?
6. What professionals are dedicated to sexual assault prevention and response?
7. What counseling services does the school have for sexual assault survivors?
8. What structures are in place to protect a victim from backlash during a pending investigation?
9. What is the school's procedure if a student reports a sexual assault?
10. What is the punishment if a student is found guilty of sexual assault?

advocate A person who works for a cause or a group.

affirmative consent A knowing, voluntary, and mutual agreement to engage in sexual activity.

burden of proof The obligation to prove one's claim.

capacity The ability or power to do, experience, or understand something.

coerce To force or threaten someone to do something they are unwilling to do voluntarily.

consensual Something that was agreed upon mutually.

consent Permission.

felony A very serious crime that is punished upon conviction with long-term jail time, a fine, or death.

forensic Scientific tests or techniques used in connection with the investigation of a crime.

impaired Being temporarily reduced in ability due to drugs, alcohol, or a medical condition such as a concussion.

incapacitated Unable to act in the interest of one's health, safety, or care for oneself, or to be unable to express a desire according to one's usual sense of reasoning because of impairment.

intoxicated To be poisoned physically, with the side effect of impaired senses and/or the loss of control over one's own behavior, usually because of alcohol or drugs.

manipulation The act of controlling or influencing a person or situation.

misdemeanor An illegal act that is considered less serious than a felony.

perpetrator Someone who has committed a crime.

plea bargain An agreement between the prosecutor and a defendant in which the defendant admits guilt in exchange for a lesser penalty.

premeditation Planning in advance.

prosecutor A lawyer who pursues charges in a legal case against a defendant in a criminal court.

psychotherapy The treatment of mental health problems by talking to a trained mental health professional.

statute of limitations The period of time in which someone can press charges or bring a legal action against another person.

Canadian Resource Centre for Victims of Crime
100–141 Catherine Street
Ottawa, ON K2P 1C3
Canada
(613) 233-7614
Website: https://crcvc.ca
This center serves as an advocate for victims and survivors of serious crimes in Canada. The staff provides a variety of support and resources for victims, including helping them deal with the criminal justice system and providing long-term emotional support.

Canadian Women's Foundation
133 Richmond St. W. Suite 504
Toronto, ON M5H 2L3
Canada
(416) 365-1444
Website: http://www.canadianwomen.org
This foundation works towards a world in which all women in Canada live free of violence, including sexual violence. They invest in violence prevention programs to teach teens about healthy and safe relationships.

It Happened to Alexa Foundation
411 Center Street
Lewiston NY, 14092
(716) 754-9105
Website: http://ithappenedtoalexa.org
This foundation works to help sexual assault victims as

they navigate the justice system by providing financial and emotional support.

National Alliance to End Sexual Violence

1129 20th Street Northwest
Suite 801
Washington, DC 20036
Website: http://endsexualviolence.org
This national alliance educates the public about legislation relating to sexual violence. It also advocates for victims of sexual violence through Congress.

National Sexual Violence Resource Center

123 North Enola Drive
Enola, PA 17025
(717) 909-0710
Website: http://www.nsvrc.org
This national center provides resources on sexual violence for individuals and organizations. The center also publishes a newsletter and organizes an annual sexual assault awareness month in April.

Pandora's Project

3109 W. 50th St.
Suite #320
Minneapolis, MN 55410-2102
Website: http://www.pandorasproject.org
This volunteer organization provides support and resources to sexual assault survivors. It provides an online support group where survivors can connect with other survivors.

RAINN (Rape, Abuse & Incest National Network)
1220 L Street NW, Suite 505
Washington, DC 20005
(800) 656-4673
Website: https://www.rainn.org/index.php
This organization partners with local agencies to pro-
    vide programs to prevent sexual violence, provide
    aid and support to victims, and ensure that those
    who commit sexual assault face justice.

WEBSITES

Because of the changing nature of internet links, Ros-
en Publishing has developed an online list of websites
related to the subject of this book. This site is updated
regularly. Please use this link to access this list:

http://www.rosenlinks.com/NTKL/consent

FOR FURTHER READING

Berlatsky, Noah. *Sexual Assault and the Military* (At Issue). Farmington Hills, MI: Greenhaven Press, 2015.

Byers, Ann. *Sexual Assault and Abuse* (Confronting Violence Against Women). New York, NY: Rosen Young Adult, 2015.

Floric, Marylee and Matthew Broyles. *Sexual Abuse* (Girls' Health). New York, NY: Rosen Central, 2011.

Ghafoerkhan, Olivia. *Sexual Assault: The Ultimate Teen Guide* (It Happened to Me). Lanham, MD: Rowman & Littlefield, 2016.

Henneberg, Susan. *I Have Been Raped. Now What?* (Teen Life 411). New York, NY: Rosen Central, 2015.

Hiber, Amanda. *Sexual Violence* (Opposing Viewpoints). Farmington Hills, MI: Greenhaven Press, 2014.

Lasky, Jack. *Sexual Assault on Campus* (Opposing Viewpoints). Farmington Hills, MI: Greenhaven Press, 2016.

Lohmann, Raychelle Cassada and Sheeta Raja. *The Sexual Trauma Workbook for Teen Girls: A Guide to Recovery from Sexual Assault and Abuse* (Instant Help Books). Oakland, CA: Instant Help Books, 2016.

May, Suellen. *Date Rape Drugs* (Understanding Drugs). New York, NY: Chelsea House Publications, 2011.

Palmer, Libbi. *The PTSD Workbook for Teens: Simple, Effective Skills for Healing Trauma.* Oakland, CA: Instant Help Books, 2012.

Anderson, Nick and Peyton M. Craighill. "College Students Remain Deeply Divided Over What Consent Actually Means." *The Washington Post*, June 14, 2015. https://www.washingtonpost.com/local /education/americas-students-are-deeply-divided -on-the-meaning-of-consent-during-sex/2015/06/11 /bbd303e0-04ba-11e5-a428-c984eb077d4e_story .html.

Anderson, Nick and Scott Clement. "1 In 5 College Women Say They Were Violated." *The Washington Post*, June 12, 2015. http://www.washingtonpost .com/sf/local/2015/06/12/1-in-5-women-say-they -were-violated.

Bennett, Jessica. "Campus Sex … With a Syllabus." *The New York Times*, January 9, 2016. http://www .nytimes.com/2016/01/10/fashion/sexual-consent -assault-college-campuses.html?_r=0.

Bidgood, Jess. "Owen Labrie of St. Paul's School Is Found Not Guilty of Main Rape Charge." *New York Times*, August 28, 2015. http://www.nytimes.com /2015/08/29/us/st-pauls-school-rape-trial-owen -labrie.html?_r=0.

Cain, Jackie. "Former North Allegheny High School Rowing Coach Gets Jail For Sex With Student, 18." WTAE.com, November 10, 2015. http://www.wtae .com/article/former-north-allegheny-high-school -rowing-coach-gets-jail-for-sex-with-student-18 /7475040.

Cevallos, Danny. "Laws on sexual consent still evolving." CNN.com, July 8, 2015. http://www.cnn.com/2015/07/08/opinions/cevallos-sex-consent-laws.

Chang, Juju et al. "The Consent Debate: College Students, Experts, Activists Discuss Sexual Consent on Campus Amid Backdrop of Alcohol and Hook-Up Culture." ABCNews.com, February 27, 2016. http://abcnews.go.com/US/consent-debate-college-students-experts-activists-discuss-sexual/story?id=37194009.

Keenan, Sandy. "Affirmative Consent: Are Students Really Asking?" *New York Times*, July 28, 2015. http://www.nytimes.com/2015/08/02/education/edlife/affirmative-consent-are-students-really-asking.html?_r=0.

Moore, Jean. "At Orientation, College Students Are Learning About Sexual Consent, Assault and How to Intervene." *Ventura County Star*, August 7, 2016. http://archive.vcstar.com/news/education/schoolwatch/at-orientation-college-students-are-learning-about-sexual-consent-assault-and-how-to-intervene-388e2-389431811.html.

Orenstein, Hannah. "California Becomes the First State to Require Teaching Consent in High School." *Seventeen*, June 17, 2016. http://www.seventeen.com/life/school/news/a41178/california-becomes-the-first-state-to-require-teaching-consent-in-high-school.

RAINN. "How Does Your State Define Consent?" March 27, 2016. https://www.rainn.org/news/how-does-your-state-define-consent.

Rubin, Bonnie Miller, "To Combat Sexual Assault, Colleges Say Yes to Affirmative Consent." *Chicago Tribune*, October 29,2015. http://www.chicagotribune.com/news/ct-college-sexual-assault-affirmative-consent-met-20151029-story.html.

"Statement on the Results of the Sexual Conduct Survey." *Harvard University*, September 21, 2015. http://www.harvard.edu/president/news/2015/statement-on-results-sexual-conduct-survey.

Viv, Stav. "New Law Sets Bar for Sexual Consent on California's Campuses." *Newsweek*, September 29, 2014. http://www.newsweek.com/new-law-sets-bar-sexual-consent-californias-campuses-274292.

Wallace, Kelly. "23% Of Women Report Sexual Assault In College, Study Finds." CNN.com, September 23, 2015. http://www.cnn.com/2015/09/22/health/campus-sexual-assault-new-large-survey.

Whitaker, Isabel Gonzales. "Vice President Joe Biden on His It's On Us Initiative to End Sexual Assault on College Campuses and Teaming Up With Lady Gaga: Exclusive." *Billboard*, March 30, 2016. http://www.billboard.com/articles/news/7317888/vice-president-joe-biden-its-on-us-initiative-interview-exclusive-lady-gaga-president-obama.

ABOUT THE AUTHOR

Carla Mooney is a graduate of the University of Pennsylvania. She is the author of many books for young adults and children. Mooney especially enjoys learning about social issues that are part of major news headlines.

PHOTO CREDITS

Cover martin-dm/E+/Getty Images; p. 5 bikeriderlondon/Shutterstock.com; pp. 7, 17, 28, 44 (background) solominviktor/Shutterstock.com; p. 8 © iStockphoto.com/Leezsnow; p. 9 Howard Kingsnorth/Cultura RM Exclusive/Getty Images; p. 14 Dean Drobot/Shutterstock.com; p. 18 Eviled/Shutterstock.com; p. 19 Aldo Murillo/E+/Getty Images; p. 21 Spencer Platt/Getty Images; p. 23 Vitchanan Photography/Shutterstock.com; p. 26 Jason and Bonnie Grower/Shutterstock.com; p. 30 Monkey Business Images/Thinkstock; p. 32 Ivan Smuk/Shutterstock.com; p. 35 © AP Images; pp. 38–39 Stephen Osman/Los Angeles Times/Getty Images; pp. 42–43 Image Source/DigitalVision/Getty Images; p. 45 Milkovasa/Shutterstock.com; p. 46 wavebreakmedia/Shutterstock.com; p. 49 Monkey Business Images/Shutterstock.com; p. 50 Nejron Photo/Shutterstock.com.

Design: Michael Moy; Layout Design: Tahara Anderson; Editor: Bernadette Davis; Photo Researcher: Sherri Jackson